SIMPLE
Prayers

Beth Lower

ELIZABETH ANN
LOWER

Simple Prayers

© 2022 Elizabeth Ann Lower

Paperback ISBN: 978-1-66783-348-4

PEOPLE

Oh, Lord, my life is so very blessed,
Through the people You send my way.
They add so much love and happiness,
To all I do each day.
You've blessed me with a family,
Who gives me love and pride.
My life is blessed through precious friends,
Who stand willingly by my side.
My church is my family, as well,
We love and support each other.
The building is not just an empty shell,
But people bound as sisters and brothers.
The love, the laughter, the stories,
The hugs, the kindness, the tears –
God, I give You all the glory,
For all the ways Your love appears.

Amen

JUDGMENT

Lord, please teach me not to judge,

Anyone who is not like me.

Sometimes I need that little nudge,

A reminder for humility.

Though we may be different from each other,

In Your eyes we are all the same.

Teach me to see all people as sisters and brothers,

You know us all by name.

Amen

GUIDANCE

Dear God, I ask You to be my guide,

As I make this journey of life.

Keep me ever by Your side,

Through the blessings, the joys, and the strife.

Guide me to take time for reflection,

As I journey through each day.

In Your word, I find direction,

To guide me along the way.

Amen

PRAYERS

God, I want to say, "Thank You", today,
For Your answers to our prayers.
The prayers sometimes only our hearts can say,
About our deepest worries and cares.
Thank You for sometimes saying, "No",
When that is for the best.
Our demands could bring confusion and woe,
But in Your will, we are blessed.
Thank You for teaching us how to pray,
"Father, Thy will be done."
We know we can stay on Your path each day,
If we will only follow the Son.
Amen

TRAVEL

Lord, as I daily travel this road,
That You have set me upon,
Guide me in giving You the load,
When I feel my strength is gone.
There are often days when my fear or pain,
Leads me close to despair.
Please remind me that in You, "all loss is gain",
Your love is as close as a prayer.
Amen

An Example

Teach me, Lord to show gratitude,
For the sunshine <u>and</u> the rain.
Keep me from a negative attitude,
When I face frustration or pain.
The comfort and love that You provide,
Are examples I can follow.
Teach me to always stay by Your side,
In joy, in laughter, in sorrow.
I want to set an example for those,
Who have never believed in You,
Teach me so my words and actions show,
All we learn from Your son is true.

Amen

Overflowing

I have so much to be thankful for,
I don't know where to start.
Thank You for opening the door,
That leads into my heart.

Amen

A PLAN

Lord, please teach me to understand,
When life doesn't go my way,
That You indeed have a master plan,
Which will be revealed one day.
Teach me to accept that hurt and sadness,
Are temporary and fleeting.
Time spent with You can restore the gladness,
Or comfort I am needing.
Teach me, Lord,
Amen

HELP

Lord, I look to You today,
To follow where You lead.
I don't have the right words to say,
To help my friend in need.
She feels so much hurt and shame,
I can't begin to understand.
But if I approach her in Your name,
Perhaps she will take my hand.
Help me, Lord.
Amen

Your Word

God, I offer thanks to You,
For the gift of Your Holy Word.
When I need guidance in what to do,
Or for my heart to be stirred.
I can read about all You have done for those,
Who gave you their faith and trust.
I know if we follow the path they chose,
You will do the same for us.
Your Holy Word can light the way,
When we are hurt or lost.
It teaches us how to live each day,
And that Jesus paid the cost.
Thank You, Lord.
Amen

Always

Teach me, Lord, that every minute,
I can go to You in prayer.
No matter what each day has in it,
You are always there.
Teach me not to put You last,
When I need a comforter or guide,
Remind me that in all days past,
You have been at my side.
Teach me, Lord.

LOST

Lord, there are times when I feel so lost,
Times when the world really pulls me down.
When my life feels like the waves that are tossed,
And hope cannot be found.
Please lead me through those hopeless days,
To the strength that You provide.
Until once again I can give You praise,
You, Lord, are my guide.
Amen

THE PATH

Guide me in my prayers, O Lord,
As daily I lift to You,
The names and concerns of all of those,
Who have asked me to.
Guide me to remember as I pray,
Thy will be done, not mine.
For when I talk with You each day,
It's your path I want to find.
Guide me to give thanks and praise,
In all my daily prayers.
You already know all my ways,
My worries and my cares.
Amen

GUIDANCE

Remind me to look for Your guidance, Lord,
In all I say and do.
Let every action or word outpoured,
Reflect and glorify You.
As I make decisions day by day,
Let Your word be my guide,
Trusting in the promises You say,
To keep me by Your side.

Amen

SERVING

I thank You, Lord, for the chances to serve,
As You have taught us to.
There are times I struggle to find the "nerve",
To tell someone about You.
But I can offer others a smile,
Or a meal that a family can share.
I can simply listen for a while,
So that person knows I care.
I may not always know what to say,
To tell others what You have done for me.
But if my actions reflect You in every way,
Those who are "blind" may someday see.

Amen

GRACE

Lord, one of the lessons I have learned,

Is that grace is given by You.

It's not something any of us can earn,

By what we say or do.

I ask You to teach me to offer grace,

When someone has left me broken.

Let Your love be reflected on my face,

Let only Your love be spoken.

Amen

CHOICES

Please guide me, God, in my choices,

Of all I do and say.

There are so many voices,

Speaking to me each day.

Voices telling me to talk about someone

When I have heard something bad.

Voices telling me, "Try this; it will be fun",

When the outcome can only be sad.

Guide me in following You each day,

As I make each choice.

I know if I listen, watch, and pray,

I will always hear Your voice. Amen

HUMILITY

Lord, please teach me to serve others,
And not look for thanks or praise.
Moments to help my sisters and brothers,
Are times I can show them Your ways.
Teach me to serve with a humble heart,
That seeks no favor nor reward.
I am so thankful to be a part,
Of Your glorious kingdom, Lord.
Amen

BEAUTY

I offer thanks, oh Lord, today,
For the beauty of this world.
As I watch baby geese at play,
And the petals of flowers unfurled.
I thank you for the colors of a summer sunrise,
For the coolness as that sun disappears.
For the power of an eagle as it flies,
And for the birdsongs that I hear.
Thank You for the majesty of mountaintops,
Reflected in crystal lakes below.
For the green and gold of abundant crops,
For the purity of fresh snow.
I am thankful for these gifts from You,
To hear, to smell, and to see.
Remind me to cherish them as You do,
And as You cherish me.
Amen

PATIENCE

God, please help me to be patient today,
To not be in a constant hurry.
When timing doesn't go my way,
I wonder, complain, and worry.
Teach me, as Mary said, to "Let it be
According to Thy will."
I can best reflect on Your love for me,
When I am quiet and still. Amen

LIGHT

As I walk, run, or sometime stumble,
In my life's journey with You,
Please remind me not to grumble,
About what I know I should do.
Guide me in making choices,
Which keep me on the narrow road.
Help me block out the negative voices,
And turn to You to help carry my load.
You have told us, "Come to Me,
And I will make your burden light."
I pray each day Your light to see,
To make my darkness bright.

Amen

GIFTS

Lord, today I give You praise,
And thank You for this life.
I am grateful for the joys You send each day,
And the shelter You offer through strife.
Thank You for the love that keeps me strong,
When the world makes me feel weak.
Your mercy keeps me from all wrong,
When it is Your path I seek.
Thank You for giving me loving friends,
And a family who adds joy to my days.
These are all gifts only You can send.
I am blessed in so many ways.
Thank You, Lord.
Amen

LESSONS

God, teach me to value each new day,
As another priceless gift.
Help me find the words to say,
To offer someone's heart a lift.
Teach me to see others as You do,
I want to serve, love, and forgive.
Teach me to become more like You,
Each day that I live.

Amen

SUN

I am grateful, Lord, for sunshine,
That brightens some difficult days.
It clears the shadows from my mind,
And breaks through the hopeless haze.
Seeing the beauty of a sunset,
Or marveling at the colors of sunrise,
Reminds me of blessings I tend to forget,
When I don't make time to "lift my eyes."
So thank You, Lord, for the beauty of the sun,
For the warmth and comfort it provides.
It reminds me from daybreak to when day is done.
You are forever at my side.
Amen

TEACH US

"Teach us to pray," the disciples asked.
Jesus taught them the Lord's Prayer.
But prayer isn't meant to be a memorized task,
Just repeating words into thin air.
Teach me to come humbly to You each day,
Ready to share my heart.
The Holy Spirit will give me the words to say,
When I don't know where to start.
Amen

GUIDANCE

Please guide me, God, each day,

As I travel this path with You.

I want to follow in Your way,

And do all that You ask me to.

Lord, at times I feel such fear,

Though I know that is not "of you",

Remind me that You are always near,

Your love is strong and true.

Guide me, Lord.

Amen

GIFTS

Thank You, God, for the gifts You give,

That add so much joy to our days.

That remind us each day that we live,

We should give You thanks and praise.

We are grateful for the family we have here on earth,

And those who are in Heaven with you.

For the joy and wonder of a baby's birth,

Your reminder that we can start anew.

Thank You for the people who touch our hearts,

For a moment, for seasons, for years,

Their presence in our lives is a precious part,

Of memories treasured and dear.

Thank You, Lord.

Amen

Tolerance

Lord, today I ask You to teach me,
To love others as You do.
To open my eyes and heart to see,
How much we are loved by You.
Though all of us are not the same,
We each play an important part.
You know all your children by our names,
Teach me to have a God-filled heart.
Amen

Darkness

Guide me through the darkness, Lord.
Guide me through my fears.
Your love is the beacon I move towards,
When I can't see through the tears.
You know my every thought and deed,
You have felt my pain.
Guide me to tell You my every need,
In You all loss is gain.
Guide me, Lord.
Amen

WORDS

Lord, please teach me self-control,
In all the words I say.
Rumors and judgment take their toll,
It's a price I don't want to pay.
Teach me to uplift those I meet,
With words of love and hope.
Make my tone and phrasing sweet,
Keep me from gossip's slippery slope.
Teach me, Lord.
Amen

TRUST

I ask You, oh God, to be my guide,
When people ask me to pray.
Let their trust in me be justified,
That I will do as they say.
There are so many who are in need,
Of the assurance of Your care.
Guide me to follow where You lead,
As I lift them to You in prayer.

Amen.

Always

I thank You, Lord, for the knowing,
You are with me in everything.
In the strong wings which are blowing,
In the beauty of the hymns we sing.
You are with me when storm clouds appear,
And seem to block the sun.
When the skies are once again clear,
And when each day is done.
I know You are with me in my sorrows,
You carry me through the pain.
I need not fear my tomorrows,
For You have promised to remain.
Thank You, Lord.
Amen

Music

Today I thank You, Lord, for all the songs,
We sing to give You praise.
The words remind us where our hearts belong,
If ever we start to stray.
Thank You for the beauty of the sound
Of old hymns and songs that are new.
We can find Your love all around,
As we lift our voices to You.

Amen

TIMING

Teach me, Lord, that Your timing,
Is always for the best.
When my worries continue climbing,
In You I can find rest.
Teach me to trust in Your perfect plan,
And that You know what I need.
I only must reach out my hand,
And follow where You lead.
Teach me, Lord.
Amen

WORDS

Lord, please guide me in the words I choose,
And when my silence is best.
Help me to discern when to share the Good News,
So others can be blessed.
I know sometimes people just need a friend,
To listen, understand, and care.
When I am the person whom you send,
Help me show my friend You are there.
Guide me, Lord.
Amen

LIFE

Lord, today I give appreciation
For all the new life You send.
Each renewal of Your creation,
Gives us the chance to start again.
Thank You. Amen

HELP

Lord, You tell us in a Bible verse,
To "love as I have loved you."
But when things go from bad to worse,
That becomes very hard to do.
Please teach me how to love someone,
Who needs more than I can provide.
Help me lead her to Your son,
So Jesus can be her guide.
Help me, Lord.
Amen

YOUR PROMISE

God, please guide my thinking,
When I start down that negative road.
When my spirits continue sinking,
When I cannot carry the load.
Guide my heart and thoughts to You,
The One who can carry all my sorrow.
There are no limits to what You can do.
And You promise a brighter tomorrow.
Guide me, Lord.
Amen

MIRACLES

Every day You touch our lives,
Through miracles big and small.
Thank You for opening our eyes,
So we can see them all.
Thank You for the miracle of laughter,
So precious when heard from a child.
And the beauty of a sunrise the morning after
A storm which was powerful and wild.
Thank You for the miracles of kindness,
Which are offered when we need them most.
Those gestures which always find us,
Pull us in and hold us close.
And thank You for the miracle You sent,
In the life of Your son Jesus.
His blood for our sins was spent.
His sacrifice truly frees us. Amen

ASKING

Lord, teach me that I can always ask,
Whatever is on my mind.
When I need strength to complete a task,
You said, "Seek, and you will find."
All my life is important to you.
No request is too small.
The Bible tells us these words are true.
I can trust my Lord with all.
Amen

Never Alone

There is so much tumult in our world today.
We are often filled with fear.
Lord, guide us to remember to stop and pray.
Remind us You are always near.
No matter what each day may bring,
You don't leave us on our own.
God, You are with us in everything.
We are never alone.
Guide us, Lord.
Amen

You Are God

Lord, there are so many things,
Which I need to be taught.
One lesson Your word clearly brings,
You are God; I am not.
Amen

Kindness

For all the kindness that You give,
Lord, I offer this thankful prayer.
For Your words which teach us how to live,
And remind us You are always there.
Thank You for the people whose earnest prayers,
Are lifted on each other's behalf.
And when life weighs us down with worries and cares,
Thank You for times we can laugh.
Amen

Enemies

Guide me to forgiveness, God.

Sometimes I lose the way.

When on my heart someone has trod,

And I don't want to pray.

When words or actions so unkind,

Cause pain for those I love,

Please gently guide my heart and mind,

To focus on You above.

Please guide me so I never forget,

Jesus died for <u>all</u> our sins.

Through the example that he set,

Enemies become friends.

Amen

Storms

In the midst of all life's storms,

Thank You, God, for being there.

When fear shows up in all its forms,

Your help is as close as a prayer.

Thank You for the promise in a rainbow,

Of your unfailing love and guidance.

It makes no difference where we go,

Your love will always find us.

Thank You, God.

Amen

GRATEFUL

Teach me, Lord, to show gratitude,
When life doesn't go as I think it should.
Give me a thankful attitude,
That all You do is for our good.
Sometimes my thoughts are dreary and bleak,
And I worry about what each day brings.
In those moments when I am fearful or weak,
Teach me to give thanks in all things.

Amen

SEEKING

Guide me in my words,
Guide me in what I do.
You love me more than the birds,
Yet they are protected, too.
Guide my heart and mind,
To do Your will each day.
You said, "Seek and you will find",
And that is what I pray.

Amen

SENSES

You made so much for us to see,
Lord, thank You for my sight.
And thank You for Jesus, who lifted me,
From darkness into light.
You made so much for us to hear.
Music, laughter, birds…
Thank You that we can know You're near,
Through listening to Your word.
You created so many textures,
We experience through touch.
Thank You for the kind gestures,
Like a hug that means so much.
All the senses You have gifted,
Bless us in so many ways.
Each day our hearts and minds are lifted,
And we give You thanks and praise.
Amen

LEARNING

Lord, there is so much I need to be taught,
So much I can't understand on my own.
I know my salvation is what Jesus bought,
And that I am never alone.
Please teach me more about how I should live,
And how to understand Your will for me.
The knowledge only You can give,
Opens my heart so I can clearly see.
Teach me, Lord.
Amen.

COMFORT ZONE

I need Your guidance Lord, today,
In serving all Your people.
I cannot do that if I stay,
In a building with a steeple.
Please guide me to those times and places,
Outside my "comfort zone".
Though I may see only unfamiliar faces,
In You, I am never alone.
Guide me, Lord.
Amen

ETERNITY

Thank You, Lord, for sending Jesus,
To die on the cross for me.
Your immeasurable sacrifice frees us,
To anticipate eternity.
Death one day will call my name,
But I will not go alone.
Death's power is what Jesus overcame,
And he will lead me home.
Thank You, Lord.
Amen

TEACHING

Lord, sometimes people aren't ready for preaching,
They just need a listening heart.
Guide me to thoughtfully follow your teaching,
And faithfully do my part.
Amen

SACRIFICE

Dear God, I offer my thanks today,
For sending us Your son.
His sacrifice has paved the way,
The battle has been won.
His miracles amazed the crowds.
The healings and the wine.
But the greatest was when he wore that shroud,
And gave his life for mine.
Thank You, God. Amen

ALWAYS

I ask You, Lord, to teach us today,
We can always depend on Your love.
Whether we bow our heads to pray,
Or look to You above.
Remind us though our doubts and sins,
Pounded in the nails,
You were loving us even then,
And Your love never fails.
Amen

STRENGTH

Lord, I ask You to be my guide,
When the days are dark and cold.
I need Your strength on my side,
I need Your hand to hold.
This journey at times is dreary and bleak,
The road seems rough and long.
Guide me in knowing though I am weak,
You are always strong.
Guide me, God.
Amen

HOPE

I want to thank You, Lord, today,
That I can give all my worries to You.
I am grateful for being able to pray,
When I don't know what to do.
The many concerns on my mind and heart,
Leave me unsure how to cope.
But prayer is where I need to start,
Your love always gives me hope.
Thank You, Lord.
Amen

DARKNESS

When the world is closing in on me,
With problems on every side,
When the road ahead I cannot see,
Please, Lord, be my guide.
Amen

CONTROL

Teach me, Lord, that what I see,
Is only a small part,
Of the great plan You have for me,
And each day is a fresh start.
Sometimes I think I know what's best,
I want to be in control.
Teach me in Your will I am blessed.
Your love makes me whole.
Amen

AMAZING

I thank You, God, for the beauty,
Of Your amazing plan.
For all the gifts You've given me,
And for sending Your love as a man.
A man who showed us how to live,
How to love, and how to pray.
A man who gave all he could give,
So we can live with You one day.
Thank You, Lord. Amen.

REST

Please teach us, Lord, every day,
To patiently seek Your will.
Teach us to take the time to pray,
Teach us to be quiet and still.
So many days we are in a hurry,
We have so much to do.
When we are weary from work and worry,
Teach us to rest in You.

Amen

QUIET

Lord, I need You to be my guide,
To keep showing me Your way.
I need to know You are by my side,
And will give me the words to say.
Sometimes I am in a hurry to talk,
I don't wait for that "still, small voice".
Guide me in my daily walk,
To make a loving choice.

Amen

THE SEED

Lord, when those I love are in deep pain,

And call on me to pray,

Sometimes "Please, Lord" is all that remains,

I don't know what else to say.

I cannot give the help they need,

I can only "come alongside."

Remind me that I can plant the seed,

You will be our Guide.

Amen

YOUR VOICE

Lord, we hear so many voices,

Telling us what to do.

They offer a tempting array of choices,

To pull us away from You.

We are told we can be prettier, richer, thinner,

Than someone on Twitter whom we "follow",

But because I know I am still a sinner,

All these promises are hollow.

Thank You for being the merciful voice,

Love and grace are what you speak.

Your path will be my only choice,

Your direction I will seek.

Thank You, Lord.

Amen

Humility

God, please teach me how to share Your grace,

With everyone I meet.

Your son knelt in that ancient place,

And washed the disciples' feet.

His lesson in being humble,

And doing that service for others,

Causes my pride to crumble.

I need to serve <u>all</u> my sisters and brothers.

Teach me, Lord.

Amen

Bad News

I ask for guidance, Lord, today.

My friend received bad news.

It's so hard to know what to say,

What direction I should choose.

Please guide me in giving my friend what she needs,

Whether it's silence, presence, or prayer.

My actions will help plant the seeds,

So she knows You are always there.

Guide me, Lord.

Amen

THE PRICE

Lord, a lesson I need to keep learning,

Each and every day,

Is that Your love isn't something I am earning.

That's a price I can never pay.

You sent Your son to pay that cost,

You let him die for me.

His sacrifice upon that cross,

Purchased my eternity.

Amen

TIMING

God, today I share my gratitude,

For knowing all things happen in Your time.

When I need to adjust an attitude,

I remember, "Not my will, but Thine."

I think about all the prayers and requests,

That reflected only my narrow view.

I am thankful that You know what is best.

All good things come from You.

Thank You, God.

Amen

Value

Today I give you thanks, Lord,
For showing me what I am worth.
Your unchanging love was outpoured,
When You sent Jesus to this earth.
The voices that tell me I don't matter,
Or that all hope is lost…
All the negative, destructive chatter,
Is silenced by the cross.
Amen

Grace

Lord, a lesson I need to learn,
To live as You want me to live,
Is that grace isn't something I can earn,
But a gift You freely give.
No petitions, sacrifice, or prayers,
No actions I have done,
Can restore me to Your loving care,
But the death of Your own son.
Teach me, Lord.

Amen

THE PATH

Dear Lord, today I am on my knees,
Asking You to be my guide.
Life brings such rough and stormy seas,
Sometimes I just want to hide.
Lead me down the path of trust.
Guide my thoughts to You above,
Nothing the world can do to us,
Can ever diminish Your love.
Guide me, Lord.
Amen

ENVY

Lord, I confess to jealousy,
When I look and I compare.
Others seem to have more than me,
And I tell myself it's not fair.
Teach me, Lord to be content,
To not complain or plead.
Jesus is the gift that You have sent,
And he is all I need.

Amen

SERVICE

Please guide me, Lord, in serving,
As the disciples were served by Your Son.
I may judge others as undeserving,
Yet You love everyone.
Guide me to reach out to those,
Who are so different from me.
Help me live so other people know,
The hope of eternity.
Guide me, Lord.
Amen

FRIENDS

Friends are truly a precious gift,
Your love expressed in a beautiful way.
They give us the courage, the hope, the "lift",
They bless our lives each day.
I thank You, God, for everyone,
Whom I can call a friend.
And the friend I have in Your precious son,
Who took away my sin.
Amen

FORGIVE

Lord, please teach me to forgive.
No matter what's been said or done,
That is how I am meant to live.
I can learn that from Your son.
When I forgive as You have forgiven me,
Your grace is what I receive.
My life will be what You want it to be,
And others may believe.
Amen

TIME

Lord, please guide me to carefully look,
At how I use my time each day.
Rather than spending hours on Facebook,
Remind me to rest and pray.
Guide me not to "follow", as many do,
On Twitter or Instagram.
My true worth is found in You,
You are the Great I Am.

Amen

Service

Lord, I am grateful for the chances You give,
To serve others in Your name.
I believe this is how You want us to live,
And one reason that Jesus came.
Thank You for the times I can share my gifts,
And touch other people's hearts.
When those around me need a "lift",
Thank You for letting me play a part.
Jesus showed us how to love and serve
How to forgive and sacrifice.
He gave so much more than we deserve,
And paid the ultimate price.
Thank You, Lord. Amen

Your Word

Lord, I give thanks for the many times,
Your Word speaks straight to my heart.
When the Scripture firmly but gently reminds,
I am expected to do my part.
Perhaps I am struggling in making a choice,
Or to find those perfect words.
In Your word, I find that "still, small voice",
The one that Elijah heard.
A voice that teaches me how to choose,
And gives me the words to say.
It shows me a love I can never lose,
No matter how far I stray.
Thank You, Lord. Amen

ACCEPTANCE

Lord, please teach us to accept Your plan,

When life doesn't go our way.

Sometimes it's hard to understand,
When we pray, and pray, and pray.
You tell us, "Ask, and ye shall receive,"

We pray, "Thy will be done."

Yet at times it's so hard to believe,

Until we focus on Your son.

Teach us, Lord.

Amen.

HURTING

Today I come to you, Lord, kneeling,

And asking You to take my hand.

The pain and loss my friends are feeling,

I cannot possibly understand.

Guide me in what help to give,

What to do, and what to say.

To gently show them their loved one still lives,

That is what I pray.

Guide me, Lord. Amen

ADVENT

I want to thank You, Lord, today,
For the season of Advent.
I know that I can never repay,
The priceless gift You sent.
Thank You, Lord.
Amen

COMPARISONS

Teach us, Lord, again and again,
That You love us all the same.
So often we make comparisons,
And want to be like "what's-his-name".
We want to be younger, richer, thinner,
Have the big house, or fancy car.
We hope to be that big lottery winner,
Or have our names known near and far.
Teach us to be more like Your son,
All he owned on earth was lost.
The eternal fame that Jesus won,
Came on an old rugged cross.
Teach us, Lord. Amen

A LESSON

Help me, Lord, to understand,
Your unrelenting grace.
Lead me to just reach out my hand,
Let my heart seek Your face.
Teach me I need not run and hide,
When I stumble or I fall.
You understand the pain that is deep inside.
Your love is there when I call.
Teach me, Lord. Amen

THE GIFT

Dear God, I thank You for the Advent season,
When we celebrate Jesus's birth.
I am so thankful Your love is the reason,
Why Jesus came to this earth.
The songs that lift our minds and hearts,
The telling of the Christmas story,
From the humble stable where it starts,
To the angels who came in glory.
Thank You for this season of hope and joy,
With all the love it brings.
I praise You for the gift of a baby boy,
Born to be our King.
Thank You, Lord.
Amen

TROUBLED TIMES

In troubled times like these, O Lord,
We ask You to be our guide.
Not just someone we look toward
But One who comes alongside.
We face new challenges every day,
And are uncertain what to do.
Guide us to faithfully follow and pray,
Your love will carry us through.

Amen

Learning

Lord, there is so much I need to learn,
And so much that You can teach.
Lessons how grace cannot be earned,
And that no one is out of reach.
Teach me how to share Your word,
So others will believe.
Let their hearts and minds be stirred,
And Your power they receive.
Teach me, Lord.
Amen

Following

Lord, I ask You to be my guide,
In knowing what someone else needs.
Help me to discard foolish pride,
And follow where You lead.
Maybe it's not a place I would choose,
Or a person who is just like me.
But it gives me the chance to share the Good News,
About my hope for eternity.
Guide me, Lord. Amen

Assurance

Thank you, God, for the assurance,
That You are "with me in all things",
No matter the occurrence,
Or what worries each day brings.
You never said that knowing You,
Would take away our problems or our fears,
But Jesus showed us Your word is true,
He assures us You are near.
Thank You, Lord. Amen

Glory

Dear God, we ask You to be our guide,
As we start each day anew.
Help us to put away selfish pride,
And give all the glory to You.
Guide us, Lord. Amen

Tolerance

Lord, please teach me to tolerate,
Those who are different from me.
It is often too easy to separate,
By beliefs or nationality.
Teach me to accept the views of others,
Though they might be different from mine.
Help me view people as sisters and brothers,
And to remember all of us are Thine.
Teach me, Lord. Amen

SEND ME

Your guidance is what I am asking today,
About where you want me to be.
As I take the time to reflect and pray,
And tell you, "Here am I; send me!"
Guide me to those times and places,
Where I can share you love in word and deed,
Where despair and grief are etched on people's faces,
I will go, Lord, if You lead.
Send me, Lord. Amen

A FRESH START

Thank You, God, for the promise and hope,
In starting a brand-new year.
Your presence and love will help us to cope,
Through every doubt and fear.
Thank You for providing a fully "clean slate",
So we can start anew.
Erasing all the guilt and hate,
And putting our trust in You.
Thank You, Lord. Amen